J & J THE KID SCIENTISTS

Explore the world of science through fun experiments at home!

J & J The Kid Scientists

ISBN: 9781736069776

Printed in the United States of America
Robinson Anderson Publishing
2150 S. Central Expressway, Suite 200
McKinney, TX. 75070

Dedication

This book is dedicated to my love bugs, my curious babies! You guys are the reason I strive to be the best in everything. I hope you both stay inquisitive. Continue to ask 50 million questions a day. Never be embarrassed to ask the what and how anything works. Always remember the best scientist started out just like you guys. Curious!

Every day that J and J wakes up, they want to begin a new scientific journey!
"Wake up Jayce! It's Saturday!" said Joshua.
"First thing first Jayce! Let's wash our faces and brush our teeth!" Cheese!!!
(smiling face)

Now, we are off to explore the world of science!
"We are the science explorers!" says Joshua.
(As he stands on top of his bed with his
chest poked out).

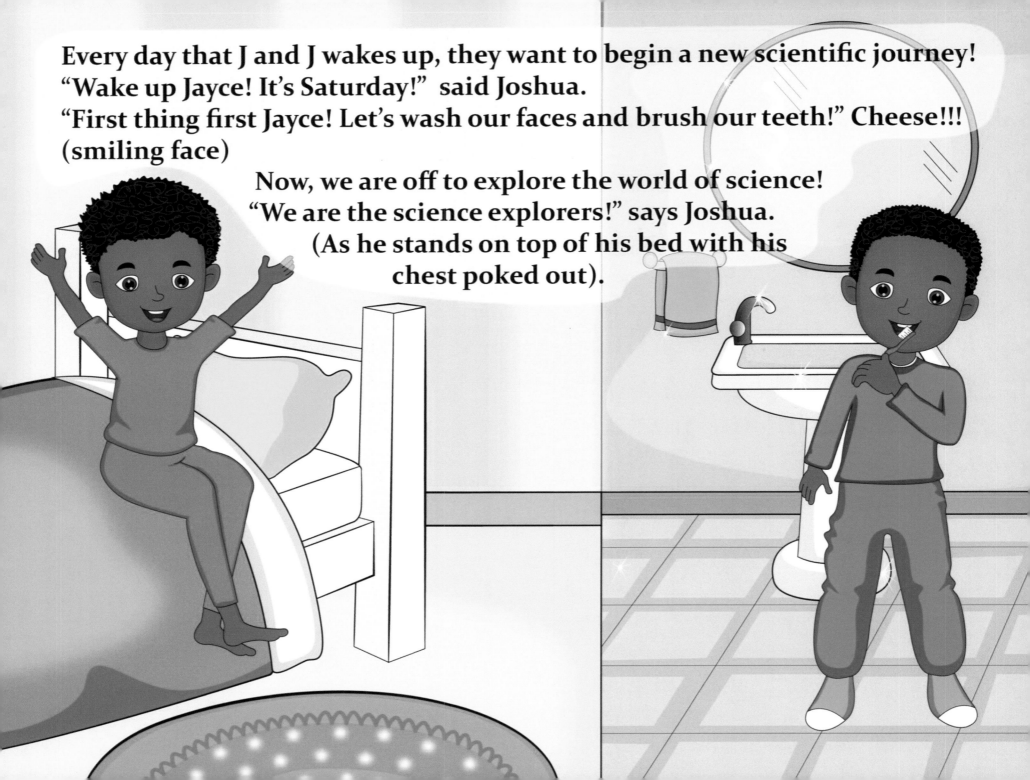

"Ok!!!" says Jayce as he hops out of bed and runs to get his safety goggles and put them on.
Booooonnnnggggg! (Eyes open largely) "How does the water come out the pipes?" asks Jayce.
The boys look at each other with sparks in their eyes and a light bulb on their forehead.

"MOMMY!!!!" Both boys scream.
"Yes boys!" their mom answered.
"Is it magic that makes water come out and splash in the sink?"
Splish splash splish (asked Joshua) Abrakadabra!!!

"Hmm?!" says mommy.
"I know I know! A man blows the water up the drain and it comes out!"
said Jayce with a burst of excitement!
"Well boys we have to do an experiment to find out how water comes out
of the drain!" says mommy.
"Yayyyyyyy!" screams both boys.
Butttt………
"First, you have to brush your teeth and wash your face." Said mommy.
"Ooookkkkayyyyy mommy!" says both boys.

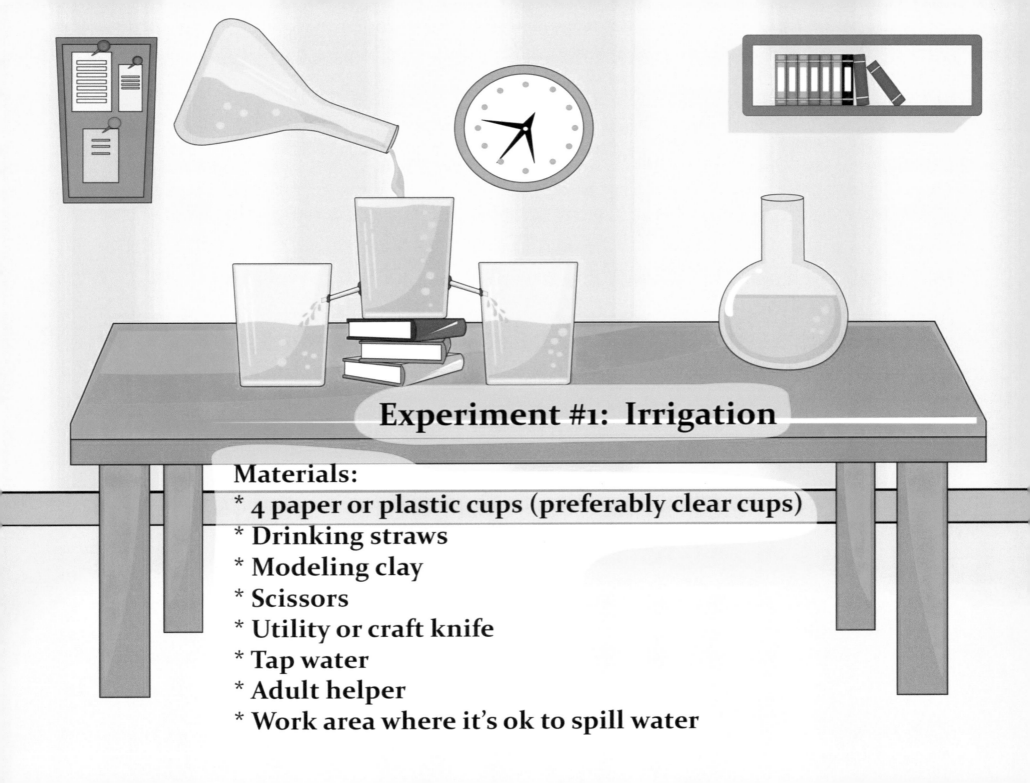

Experiment #1: Irrigation

Materials:
* 4 paper or plastic cups (preferably clear cups)
* Drinking straws
* Modeling clay
* Scissors
* Utility or craft knife
* Tap water
* Adult helper
* Work area where it's ok to spill water

Preparation:

An adult helper use the knife to make two small x shaped slits about 1/3 of the way down from the top of a cup on opposite sides of the cup

Get two more cups and make one x shape slit in each cup about 1/3 of the way up from the bottom, but slightly lower than the slits in the first cup. The slits in the first cup should be higher than the slits in the second two cups.

Poke one drinking straw through each slit in the first cup. Then poke the other ends of the straws through the slits in the other cups.

Use small pieces of modeling clay to form a seal around the straws inside each cup to prevent water from leaking out around it.
*If the cups are not sitting flat. Put a few coins in the bottom of the cups to help weigh them down.

Slowly pour water into the central cup. When the water reaches the straw, you will see water disperse to the other cups.

After eating breakfast, the science explorers began to play.
Boom crash pow the sound of laughter
and car wheels screeching and the pitter
patter of feet running around and around
filled the house. Joshua and Jayce do
a mad dash to the kitchen and crash into t
heir mommy. Joshua says, "Mommy I'm
thirsty like a camel!"
Jayce said, "Yeah I'm thirsty like a plant!"
Joshua laughed and in confusion said,
"Like a plant?"

Both boys turn to their mommy and asked,
"How do plants drink?"

"Well boys I would tell you, but I think
you will understand better if I show you."
"Yay!!!" said both boys.

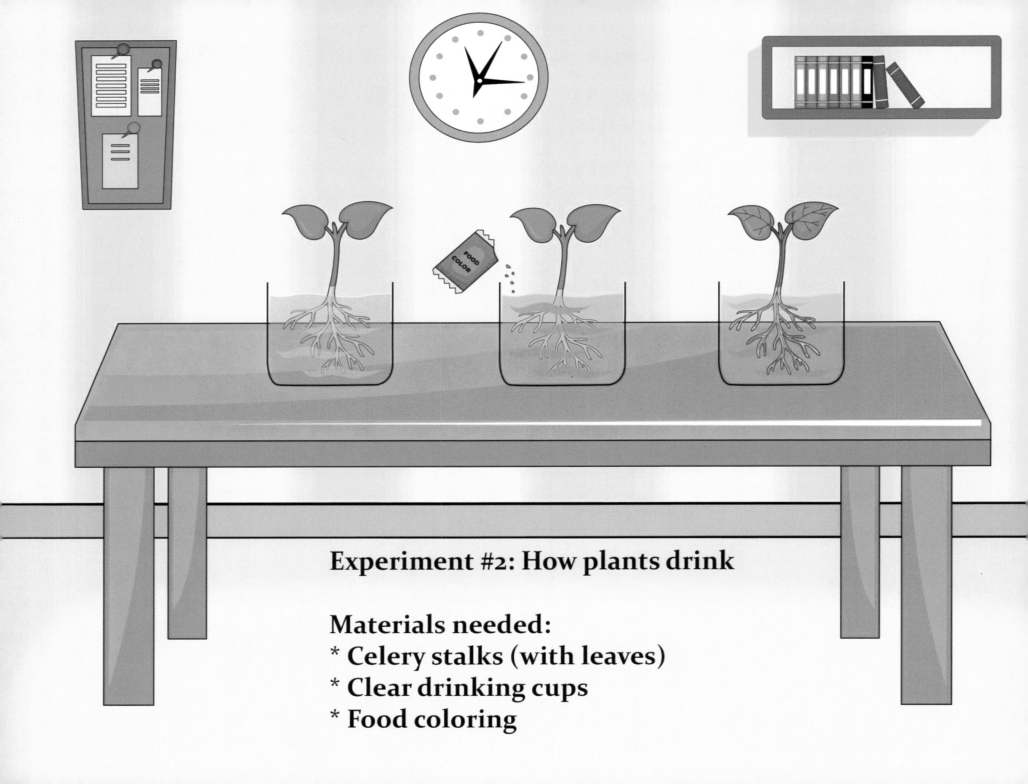

Experiment #2: How plants drink

Materials needed:
* Celery stalks (with leaves)
* Clear drinking cups
* Food coloring

Preparation:

Celery stalks that have leaves at the top work best. The stalks on the inside of the bundle of celery usually have the most leaves.

Cut about an inch or so off the bottom of the celery stalks.

Fill each container about halfway with water and drop 10-15 drops of food coloring in each clear drinking cup. Place the celery stalks in the water.

Observe the celery at the end of the school day. You may see a little color in the stalk or the leaves. Observe them again the next day and you should see color in the leaves. After 48 hours you will really notice changes and color in the stalks and leaves showing that the water traveled up through the stalk to the leaves.

Now that everyone has eaten, we need to get moving.
We have a lot of places to go today.
"It's time to get dressed," says daddy. "J & J, what should we find out first
that will help us pick out appropriate clothes?"

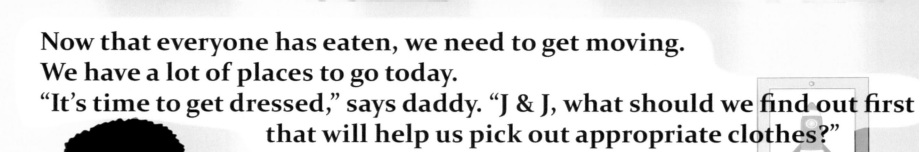

Hmm let's think about that........
"I know I know," ... says Joshua (jumping up and down excitedly).
"We check the weather."
"Yes, we can look outside the window and search for the sun!"
says Jayce.
"Yes, both of you are correct!" said daddy.

"Well boys let's go get the thermometer you made with Gam-Gam (grandma) to check the temperature!" says daddy.

Both boys yell together! "Let's go get it! I bet you I will find it first," says Joshua! Jayce screams, "No I will"............... while zipping down the hallway.

Boom pow crash is what you hear coming from their bedrooms.

"Ah ha! I have it." says Jayce. "Hurry! Let's go outside on the back porch and check the weather. Our thermometer shows it is hot today!" said Joshua. "Whew, it sure is!" said Jayce as he wiped the sweat from his forehead. "I'm going to wear a T-shirt and shorts," says Jayce. "Great idea!" says Joshua.

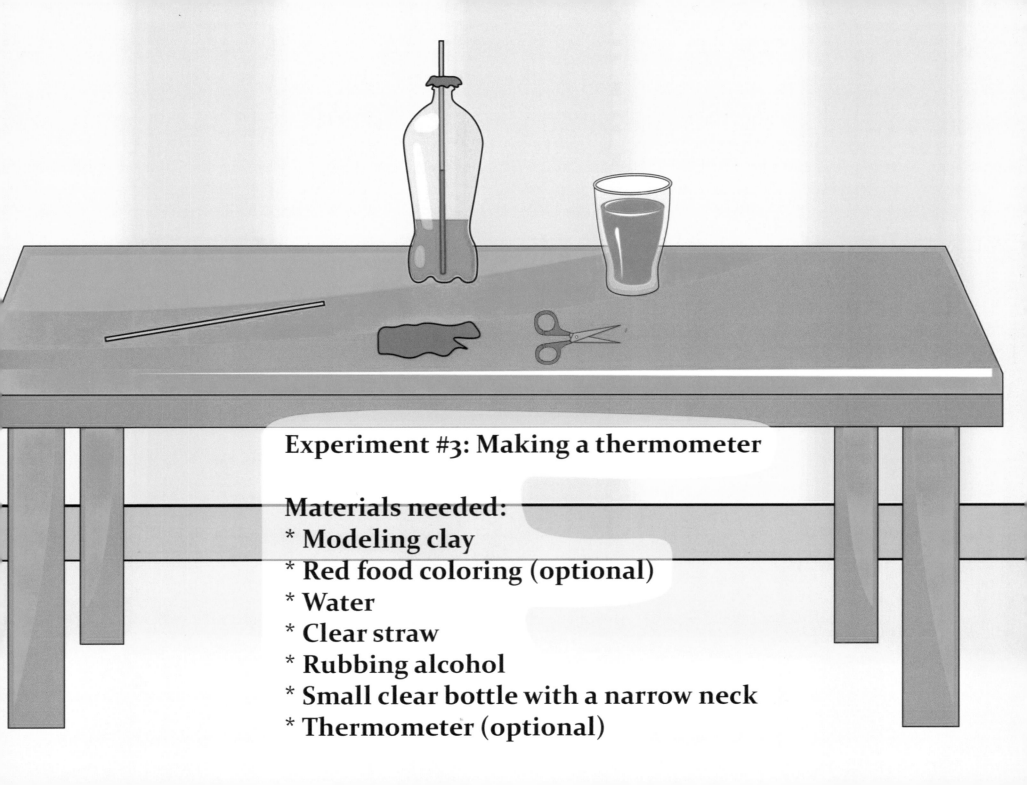

Experiment #3: Making a thermometer

Materials needed:
* **Modeling clay**
* **Red food coloring (optional)**
* **Water**
* **Clear straw**
* **Rubbing alcohol**
* **Small clear bottle with a narrow neck**
* **Thermometer (optional)**

Pour equal amounts of water and rubbing alcohol into the bottle until it is 1/4 of the way full. Add in a few drops of red food coloring to make it more visible and to look like a thermometer.

Put the straw into the bottle and wrap the clay tightly around it and the opening of the bottle. You do not want the straw touching the bottom of the bottle, so move it up and have the clay hold it in place. Leave the top opening of the straw uncovered.

Now you can test the thermometer! Put your hands around it to see if that warms it up.

You get a small reaction with the heat from your hands.

Or place it into a bowl of hot water to get a fast reaction. You can see when we put it into hot water to rise above the clay!

Now try putting it into the freezer to see what change happens.
Test it outside in your weather on a hot or cold day and see what happens.

"Now that we have on appropriate clothes and shoes for the weather, let's get in the car and go!" Says mommy.

"Yayyy. I'm going to count as many green cars I see,"! says Jayce.

"I'm going to count as many blue cars I see," says Joshua.

"Mommy, are you going to count the pink cars you see?" asked Joshua?

"Yes, son I will," said Mommy

"Daddy, are you going to look for red cars?" asked Jayce.

"Yes, I will son,". said daddy.

"Hey, what makes cars go?" Jayce asked.

"Jayce, daddy pushes a button and the car goes!" Joshua says. Zoom zoom vrrrooom vroom ...

"Not quite boys. I can tell you but I think it will be fun to show you. When we get back home we can do a quick experiment." said Daddy.

"Yayyyy I can't wait to come back home!".

Both boys scream with excitement at the same time!

After leaving the gas station, grocery store, car wash and singing several versions of the wheels on the bus, we are finally heading home.

Mommy says. "Boys I have a question. What do you think we will make our car experiment with?"

"We can use different shapes like circles for the tires and something square for the car," says Joshua.

"Mommy, we can use my legos to build a car, right daddy?". says Jayce.

"You are right fellas; we can build a car using a lot of things we have at home." says daddy.

Mommy agreed. "Yes we can!"

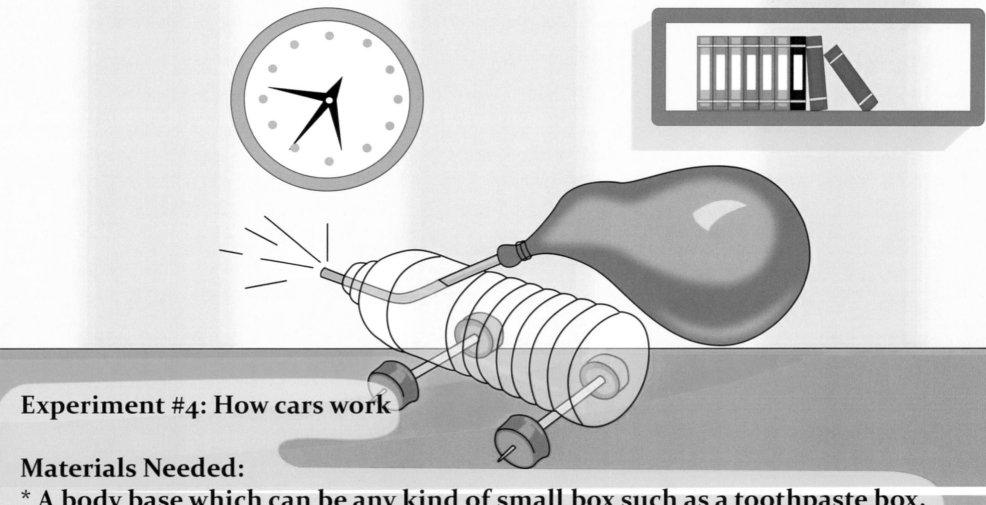

Experiment #4: How cars work

Materials Needed:
* A body base which can be any kind of small box such as a toothpaste box,
or * One 20oz. bottle
* Four water bottle caps that can be easily pierced
* Two skinny sticks that can fit through a straw
* Two straws
* One large balloon
* Plenty of strong tape

Directions:
Step 1: Cut two sticks to about 3 inches long
Step 2: Cut two straws to about 2 inches long
Step 3: Use scissors to cut a small slit in each of the four bottle caps
Step 4: Push a stick through ONE of the bottle cap's slits so that about 1/2 in. is sticking out on one side and 3.5 inches are sticking out on the other side
Step 5: Before sticking another bottle cap on the other side of the twig, put the straw on the longer part of the stick and then finish it off with the other bottle cap about one half of the other end of the stick.
Step 6: To finish off the axle, put a bit of tape attaching the bottle cap to the stick but not the straw. You will notice that you can hold onto the straw and rotate the rest of the axle.
Step 7: Repeat steps 4-6 so that two axles are made for the soon to be balloon car

Attaching the base to the axles:
Step 1: About 1/3 of the way into the base that you have chosen (toothpaste box in this case) tape ONLY the straw to the bottom of the base.
Step 2: Attach the other axle 1/3 of the way from the other end of the base.
Step 3: Consider aerodynamics when you choose which side of the base will be the front and back.

Attaching the accelerator:

Step 1: Stick about an inch of a straw into the balloon and tape the balloon onto the straw. Try not to tape too much of the balloon but make sure that it is stabilized onto the straw well. Make sure that the balloon is NOT like the one in the picture and hanging off of the edge of the base. This will cause the balloon to drag on the floor and restrict its movement.

Step 2: Next tape the part of the straw that is closest to the balloon onto the top of the base. The top of the base is the side that is the opposite of the one with the axles on it.

Now your car is ready to be driven!! Blow air into the straw that is attached to the balloon so that the balloon fills up with air. Place it on a flat surface and watch it go!!!

Whew.... we learned a lot today and had so much fun.
"Boys, what did you learn today?" asked mommy.
"Everything has to drink water to grow, even plants," says Jayce.
"Aaaannnnddddd we should always check the weather before we
put on our clothes. Aaaannnnddddd ...."

Joshua interrupts. "We learned how water flows from one place to another.
What do we call that mommy?" Irrigation says mommy.

"Well boys, it's time to rest our brains and go to sleep." says mommy.
"Goodnight fellas." says daddy while giving both boys a secret handshake.

"Say your prayers and we will see you in the morning loves." says mommy.
The boys scream, "Goodnight!"

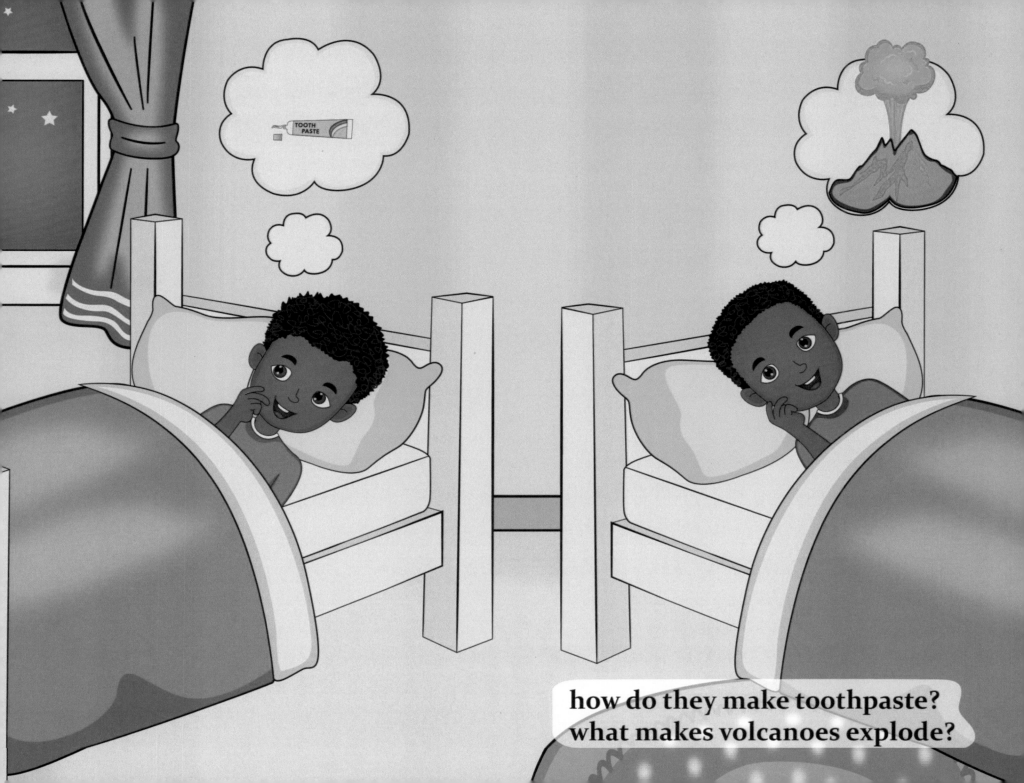

Citations

Irrigation experiment
https://www.scientificamerican.com

Plants drinking water experiment
http://www.weareteachers.com

Balloon powered car
http://www.instructables.com

Thermometer experiment
http://www.teachbesideme.com

CPSIA information can be obtained
at www.ICGtesting.com
Printed in the USA
BVRC101623131221
623918BV00003B/48